Toys I play with

Let's pretend

Barbara Hunter

Little Nippers

www.heinemann.co.uk/library
Visit our website to find out more information about **Heinemann Library** books.

To order:
☎ Phone 44 (0) 1865 888066
▤ Send a fax to 44 (0) 1865 314091
💻 Visit the Heinemann Bookshop at www.heinemann.co.uk/library to browse our catalogue and order online.

First published in Great Britain by Heinemann Library, Halley Court, Jordan Hill, Oxford OX2 8EJ, part of Harcourt Education.
Heinemann is a registered trademark of Harcourt Education Ltd.

Editorial: Jilly Attwood and Claire Throp
Design: Jo Hinton-Malivoire and bigtop, Bicester, UK
Models made by: Jo Brooker
Picture Research: Catherine Bevan
Production: Lorraine Warner

Originated by Dot Gradations
Printed and bound in China by South China Printing Company

ISBN 0 431 16344 8 (hardback)
06 05 04 03 02
10 9 8 7 6 5 4 3 2 1

ISBN 0 431 16349 9 (paperback)
06 05 04 03 02
10 9 8 7 6 5 4 3 2 1

British Library Cataloguing in Publication Data
Hunter, Barbara
Let's pretend. – (Toys I play with)
790.1'33
A full catalogue record for this book is available from the British Library.

Acknowledgements
The publishers would like to thank the following for permission to reproduce photographs:
Gareth Boden.

Cover photograph reproduced with permission of Tudor Photography

The publishers would like to thank Annie Davy for her assistance in the preparation of this book.

Every effort has been made to contact copyright holders of any material reproduced in this book. Any omissions will be rectified in subsequent printings if notice is given to the publishers.

Contents

Shopkeepers

POST OFFICE

It's fun to pretend to work in a shop or post office.

Chef

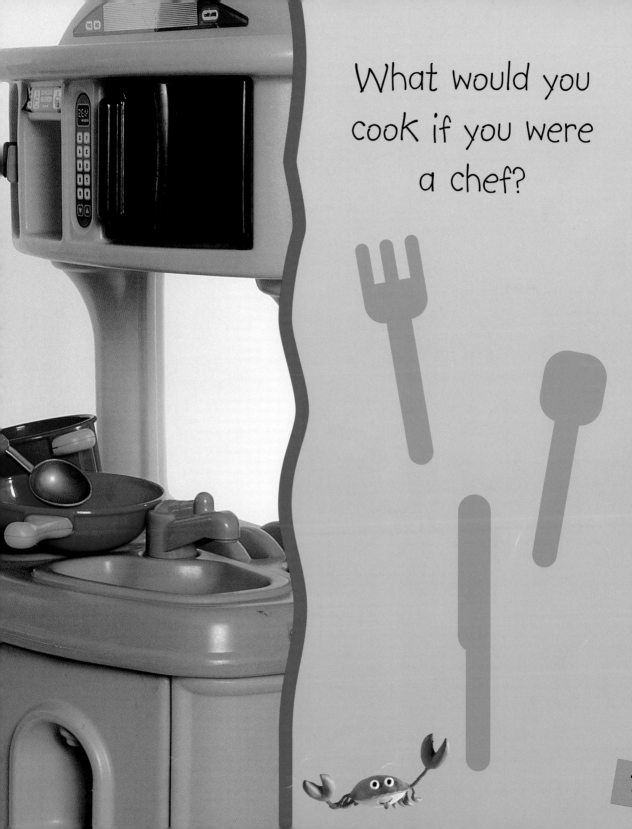

What would you cook if you were a chef?

7

Builder

You can hammer and saw just like a builder.

What tools are these?

screwdriver

hammer

saw

spanner

9

Doctors or nurses

You can try to make your sick toys better.

They need lots of looking after.

Vet

Pets need
looking after too.

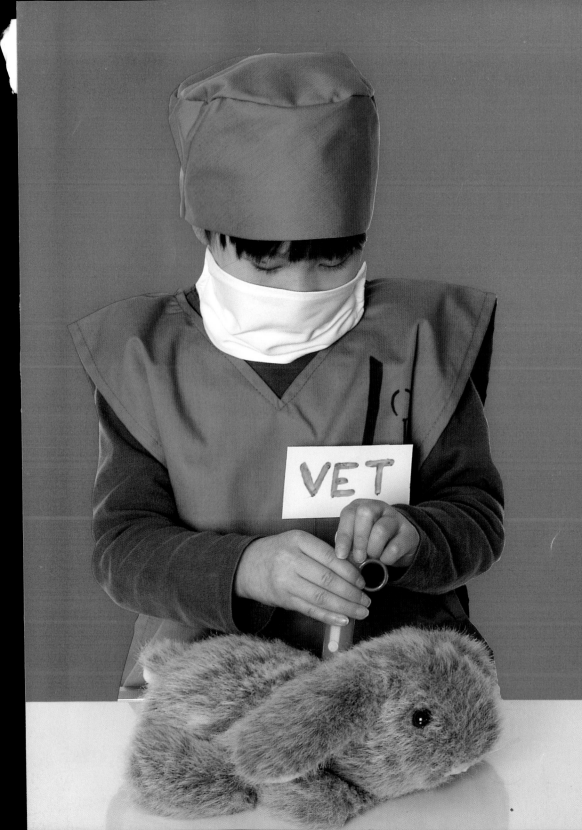

Teacher

Heading

a b c

Toys

IMAGES

Toys
Karen Bryant-Mole

14

If you are a teacher you writing need to make sure all the class are listening!

17

Clown and pirate

You can dress up and pretend you are a clown at the circus.

You can be a pirate
out at sea.

Or do you want to be a prince or princess?

You could dress
up in a robe
and crown.

21

Let's pretend toys

Crown

Saucepans

Helmet

23

Index

The end

Notes for adults

This series supports the young child's knowledge and understanding of their world. The following Early Learning Goals are relevant to the series.
• Find out about, and identify, some features of living things, objects and events that they observe.
• Exploration and investigation: feeling textures and materials.

The series explores a range of different play experiences by looking at features of different toys and the materials they are made from. **Let's Pretend Toys** includes things made from the following materials: plastic, metal, paper, fabric, wood and cardboard. Some of the experiences featured in this book include dressing up, creating an imaginary world, being 'grown-up' and having a job which often involves helping others.

There is an opportunity for the child to compare and contrast different roles played by 'characters' as well as relating them to their own experiences, e.g. they may be familiar with playing at being 'a doctor' or 'a vet', but being 'a chef' or 'post office clerk' may be new to them.

Follow-up activities
By making direct reference to the book the child can be encouraged to try new experiences such as dressing up and role playing unusual characters, e.g. a firefighter/police officer/pirate. Taking photographs of the activities would be an excellent way for the child to start making their own book.